Other books in the series:
The Crazy World of Birdwatching (Peter Rigby)
The Crazy World of Cats (Bill Stott)
The Crazy World of Cricket (Bill Stott)
The Crazy World of Gardening (Bill Stott)
The Crazy World of Golf (Mike Scott)
The Crazy World of the Handyman (Roland Fiddy)
The Crazy World of Jogging (David Pye)
The Crazy World of Love (Roland Fiddy)
The Crazy World of Marriage (Bill Stott)
The Crazy World of Music (Bill Stott)
The Crazy World of the Office ((Bill Stott)
The Crazy World of Photography (Bill Stott)
The Crazy World of the Royals (Barry Knowles)
The Crazy World of Rugby (Bill Stott)
The Crazy World of Sailing (Peter Rigby)
The Crazy World of School (Bill Stott)
The Crazy World of Sex (David Pye)
The Crazy World of Skiing (Craig Peterson & Jerry Emerson)
The Crazy World of Tennis (Peter Rigby)

Published in Great Britain in 1990 by
Exley Publications Ltd, 16 Chalk Hill,
Watford, Herts WD1 4BN, United Kingdom.

Copyright © Bill Stott 1990
Second and third printings 1991

A copy of the CIP data is available from the
British Library on request.

ISBN 1-85015-241-1

Printed and bound in Hungary.

the CRAZY world of HOSPITALS

Cartoons by Bill Stott

▤ EXLEY

"You know, for a moment there, I got the distinct impression that you didn't want me to take these off."

"Poor Mr. Hardacre's got to have another enema ..."

"A little tense today, Mr. Fairbrother?"

"*I've had a terrible time. I was so ill, I didn't even want to talk about it!*"

"... and the lady at Number 47 with the big chests has made Daddy three cakes and one of those lasagnes you hate ..."

"*I've told you before – no more wheelies!*"

"You'll have to speak up – 'piles' did you say?"

"Nothing wrong with your reflexes ..."

"Now, you'll just feel a slight ..."

*"One of the hidden pitfalls of private medicine, I'm afraid –
I've found out what's wrong with you, but I won't tell you
unless you pay double."*

"They only ever cry at visiting time …"

"Valve's stuck ..."

"Fifty years married and never a night of fun – until now!"

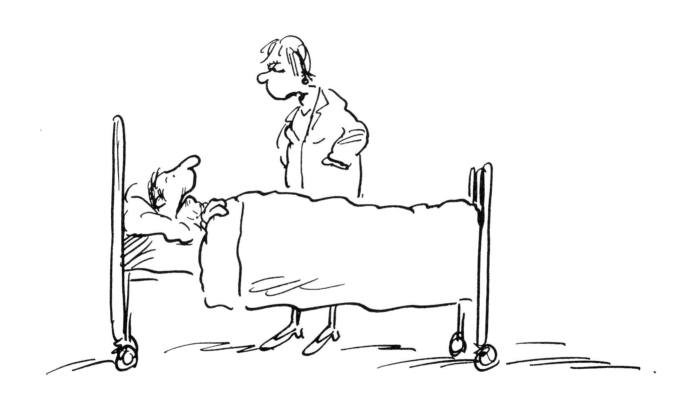

"Well, we've had the results of the tests Mr. Fittock and I have to tell you that you have nothing famous."

"Well, it was a sort of white-hot agony searing my whole being to the point of unconsciousness. Now it's receding like a purple curtain of pain, a sweeping tide of physical discomfort reforming, preparing for the next awful onslaught."

"Here's a list of things to talk about for tomorrow. Learn it."

"Hi there, I'm Chief Surgeon Tom Berkowicz. I'll be taking care of your little op. Today, on scalpels is Jennifer Webb. Looking after swabs is Nurse Jimmy Peters. Vital signs are ..."

"And whose idea was it to bring Aunt Eileen?"

"Have you got that one by our catering manager – 'Lives of the Great Poisoners'?"

"If you don't let me give you this suppository, I'll tell nurse what you said about her walk."

"I don't trust these surgeons – so I make them keep everything they take out."

"Doctor – about the youth brought in after being cut free from the park railings ..."

"For heaven's sake, Mr. Willoughby, you're only having your verruca trimmed!"

"Age? You mean now or when we first sat down?"

AND THEN ON MONDAY
MRS WHATSERNAME RANG
AND ASKED AFTER YOU JUST
BEFORE DOREEN CALLED AND
GUESS WHAT? THEIR GARY
HAS FINALLY ......
ZZZZZZZZZZZZZZZZ

"That Mr. Stephenson is out of bed again. If he's smoking in the toilet, I'll ..."

"My social life affecting my work? What makes you say that, Nurse?"

Nurse Stebbings. Mr. Finch is excused bed-baths."

"Those? Banister rails. He didn't want to come."

"There's been some sort of mistake. He came to clean the windows."

"I know just the operation for you, Mr. Spendlove. Unfortunately, I don't think anybody has pulled off a whole body transplant yet."

"If we gave you <u>nice</u> food, you'd want to stay here instead of going home to your loved ones."

"I've been waiting so long, my stomach pains have cleared up. I've got a headache now."

"When I said 'use your imagination' about bringing my clothes in, I did not mean one pair of dungarees, two left boots and a ski hat."

"That Mrs. Goodbody around the corner's having <u>another</u> dedication on the hospital radio."

"Two visitors per bed …"

"That Nurse O'Hooligan hates visitors who pretend not to have heard the bell."

"This bleeper's got a mind of its own."

"*I know you feel sorry for Mr. Finningsby, but putting sandwiches in his ear really doesn't help.*"

"I told you it was a hair piece!"

"Now then – you're not frightened of me are you, little man?"

"Put that down as 'no', Nurse."

"Yes – that's my surgeon – the one who cuts himself shaving ..."

"He criticizes everything – the food, the staff – everything.
So I've put him on the critical list."

"What do you mean, you hate the smell of hospitals? You're the doctor!"

"George! It's a lady doctor ..."

"Didn't I tell you? That young blonde doctor
hates chauvinist remarks."

"Keep your eye on him: it's not every day you operate on your bank manager."

"Brace yourself, son. When J.J. Farnsworth lances a boil – he lances a boil!"

"He's got his father's nose."

"Nurse Willoughby! During a bed-bath, only the patient is in the bed!"

"Doctor, Doctor, Mr. Brunskill's showing off again."

"It's a type of suspended animation. We call it 'waiting'."

"Yes, it is unfortunate – just don't go in any tough areas."

"Come on, own up. <u>How</u> fast were you wheeling Mr. Goodacre?"

"I thought before we chatted you could run through the washing machine manual with me ..."

"Name?"

"Before I leave you to soak, Mr. Worthington, let me remind you that only at Sunnyview Private Clinic do you get boats in the bath."

"I can understand you feeling jealous of Mr. Pratt's hardware, but it wouldn't do your strangulated hernia any good at all."

"*My colleagues and I are baffled. We have no idea what's wrong with you – but would you mind nipping up to the children's ward – they love a good laugh.*"

"She's still not herself – she had me put the grapes in water and then ate the daffodils ..."

"I've bitten the ends off more thermometers than you've had hot dinners tootsie."

"Well, it's not a *good* sign, that's for sure ..."

"Early morning alarm call Doctor?"

"I think that's enough chit-chat for now, Mrs. Spiggot."

"We don't know what it is, but we do know it's contagious."

Books from the "Crazy World" series:

The Crazy World of Birdwatching. £3.99. By Peter Rigby. Over seventy cartoons on the strange antics of the twitcher brigade. One of our most popular pastimes, this will be a natural gift for any birdwatcher.

The Crazy World of Cats. £3.99. By Bill Stott. Fat cats, alley cats, lazy cats, sneaky cats – from the common moggie to the pedigree Persian – you'll find them all in this witty collection. If you've ever wondered what your cat was really up to, this is for you.

The Crazy World of Cricket. £3.99. By Bill Stott. This must be Bill Stott's silliest cartoon collection. It makes an affectionate present for any cricketer who can laugh at himself.

The Crazy World of Gardening. £3.99. By Bill Stott. The perfect present for anyone who has ever wrestled with a lawnmower that won't start, over-watered a pot plant or been assaulted by a rose bush from behind.

The Crazy World of Golf. £3.99. By Mike Scott. Over seventy hilarious cartoons show the fanatic golfer in his (or her) every absurdity. What really goes on out on the course, and the golfer's life when not playing are chronicled in loving detail.

The Crazy World of the Handyman. £3.99. By Roland Fiddy. This book is a must for anyone who has ever hung *one* length of wallpaper upside down or drilled through an electric cable. A gift for anyone who has ever tried to "do it yourself" and failed!

The Crazy World of Love. £3.99. By Roland Fiddy. This funny yet tender collection covers every aspect of love from its first joys to its dying embers. An ideal gift for lovers of all ages to share with each other.

The Crazy World of Marriage. £3.99. By Bill Stott. The battle of the sexes in close-up from the altar to the grave, in public and in private, in and out of bed. See your friends, your enemies (and possibly yourselves?) as never before!

The Crazy World of Music. £3.99. By Bill Stott. This upbeat collection will delight music-lovers of all ages. From Beethoven to Wagner and from star conductor to the humblest orchestra member, no-one escapes Bill Stott's penetrating pen.

The Crazy World of the Office. £3.99. By Bill Stott. Laugh your way through the office jungle with Bill Stott as he observes the idiosyncrasies of bosses, the deviousness of underlings and the goings-on at the Christmas party.... A must for anyone who has ever worked in an office!

The Crazy World of Photography. £3.99. By Bill Stott. Everyone who owns a camera, be it a Box Brownie or the latest Pentax, will find something to laugh at in this superb collection. The absurdities of the camera freak will delight your whole family.

The Crazy World of Rugby. £3.99. By Bill Stott. From schoolboy to top international player, no-one who plays or watches rugby will escape Bill Stott's merciless exposé of their habits and absurdities. Over seventy hilarious cartoons – a must for addicts.

The Crazy World of Sailing. £3.99. By Peter Rigby. The perfect present for anyone who has ever messed about in boats, gone pea-green in a storm or been stuck in the doldrums.

The Crazy World of the School. £3.99. By Bill Stott. A brilliant and hilarious reminder of those chalk-throwing days. Wince at Bill Stott's wickedly funny new collection of crazy school capers.

The Crazy World of Sex. £3.99. By David Pye. A light-hearted look at the absurdities and weaker moments of human passion – the turn-ons and the turn-offs. Very funny and in (reasonably) good taste.

The Crazy World of Skiing. £3.99. By Craig Peterson and Jerry Emerson. Covering almost every possible (and impossible) experience on the slopes, this is an ideal present for anyone who has ever strapped on skis – and instantly fallen over.

The Crazy World of Tennis. £3.99. By Peter Rigby. Would-be Stephen Edbergs and Steffi Grafs watch out! This brilliant collection will pin-point their pretensions and poses. Whether you play yourself or only watch on TV, this will amuse and entertain you!

These books make super presents. Order them from your local bookseller or from Exley Publications Ltd, Dept BP, 16 Chalk Hill, Watford, Herts WD1 4BN. (Please send £1.50 for one book or £2.25 for two or more to cover postage and packing.)